131865 EN
Marine Biologist

Somervill, Barbara A.
ATOS BL 6.3
Points: 1.0   MG

21st
Century
Skills Library

COOL SCIENCE CAREERS

MARINE BIOLOGIST

BARBARA A. SOMERVILL

Published in the United States of America by
Cherry Lake Publishing, Ann Arbor, Michigan
www.cherrylakepublishing.com

Content Adviser
David L. Taylor, Assistant Professor, Department of Biology and Marine Biology,
Roger Williams University

Credits
Photos: Cover and page 1, ©Zagor/Dreamstime.com; page 4, ©Qldian/
Dreamstime.com; page 6, ©PhotoSky 4t com, used under license from
Shutterstock, Inc.; page 9, ©Rickdrew/Dreamstime.com; page 10, ©Mira/Alamy;
page 12, ©Mark Boulton/Alamy; page 15, ©David R. Frazier Photolibrary, Inc./
Alamy; page 16, ©David Levenson/Alamy; page 19, ©Mark Conlin/Alamy; page 21,
© David Wootton/Alamy; page 22, ©Jiayikang/Dreamstime.com; page 24,
©Michael Patrick O'Neill/Alamy; page 27, ©Horizon International Images Limited/
Alamy; page 28, ©Images&Stories/Alamy.

Library of Congress Cataloging-in-Publication Data
Somervill, Barbara A.
  Marine biologist / by Barbara A. Somervill.
    p. cm.—(Cool science careers)
  Includes index.
  ISBN-13: 978-1-60279-504-4
  ISBN-10: 1-60279-504-5
  1. Marine biologists—Vocational guidance—Juvenile literature. I. Title.
II. Series.
  QH91.45.S66 2009
  578.77023—dc22   2008045234

Cherry Lake Publishing would like to acknowledge
the work of The Partnership for 21st Century Skills.
Please visit *www.21stcenturyskills.org* for more information.

TABLE OF CONTENTS

CHAPTER ONE
AN UNDERWATER WORLD

Two marine biologists adjust their diving masks. They give a thumbs-up to show they're ready. Then they jump into the water. They are diving in Mexico's Sea of

Without the help of marine biologists, hammerhead sharks and other animals could become extinct.

Cortez to study hammerhead sharks. Thousands of these sharks once swarmed in the area. Today, the number of hammerheads there is decreasing. Overfishing has destroyed the **ecosystem**. Hundreds of young hammerheads are lost each year. The marine biologists say that fishers must stop targeting the sharks. They work with the Mexican government, **fishery** managers, and **conservation** groups to save the ecosystem.

Marine biologists are part of a new, growing field of study called marine conservation **biology**. Experts in this field work to save ocean life. They want to preserve the **habitats** of Earth's oceans and seas. Marine biologists study the ocean's surface and its deepest depths. High-tech instruments and inventions allow marine scientists to study new creatures in new places. But marine biologists aren't the first people to study ocean life.

Aristotle (384–322 BCE) was one of the world's most famous philosophers. He lived in ancient Greece near the Aegean Sea and studied sea life. He described many species of **crustaceans**, fish, and other marine life.

Over the next 2,000 years, scientists, scholars, and sailors continued to study marine life. But their studies were limited. They collected, named, and studied the sea creatures and plants that they could find. But what about life beyond their reach? Humans could not go as far down into the water as many fish and marine mammals could. People needed some type of diving equipment that would allow them to breathe underwater. Inventors developed early diving suits. These models were heavy and not very safe. Divers breathed through rubber hoses attached to air pumps on the ship. One tear in the hose, and the diver might die. Marine biologists had to limit their studies to shallow coastal waters.

Modern diving equipment helps marine biologists dive deeper than they could in the past.

In the 19th and 20th centuries, new inventions led to many advances in marine science. Ships such as the USS *Albatross* were equipped with scientific laboratories. Crews dragged nets along the seafloor to collect samples of marine life. Marine biologists studied the creatures that were brought up from the sea.

LEARNING & INNOVATION SKILLS

The aqualung allowed a diver to breathe air from a tank through a special valve. It was an early form of today's self-contained underwater breathing apparatus (scuba). Improvements to scuba equipment have allowed marine biologists to closely study things such as **coral reefs**.

Experts develop better diving gear by identifying problems with current models. Today, marine biologists use **rebreathers**. They make fewer bubbles and less noise than scuba gear. Why do you think it was important for experts to come up with diving equipment that made less noise?

In 1943, a new invention allowed scientists to swim with the fishes they studied. Frenchmen Jacques Cousteau and

Émile Gagnan developed the aqualung. Aqualungs allowed marine biologists to dive for longer periods of time. They could dive deeper and learn more about the sea than ever before.

LIFE & CAREER SKILLS

Captain Jacques-Yves Cousteau worked with Émile Gagnan to create the aqualung. That was not the only thing Cousteau was known for, though. He was also a well-known explorer, researcher, and filmmaker. He became famous for his television documentaries, making more than 120 of them during his lifetime.

In 1973, Cousteau founded the Cousteau Society. The main goal of the Cousteau Society is to educate people about aquatic life. Hopefully, this will lead people to care more about protecting Earth's waters. Today, the society has more than 50,000 members.

Today, marine science reaches deep into the ocean. Scientists travel in **submersible** vehicles. Or they send remotely operated vehicles to the ocean floor. Technology

Submarines are important tools for marine biologists who study the depths of the ocean.

has changed how and where marine biologists do their work. But one thing remains the same—the wonder of exploring new places and finding new species.

CHAPTER TWO
STUDYING SEA LIFE

There are thousands of marine biologists, but that's not always what they are called at their jobs. These experts might be called oceanographers (scientists who study oceans) or any

A group of marine biologists studies sea turtle hatchlings on a beach.

one of a dozen other titles. Marine biologists study tide pools, seaweed, crustaceans, and marine mammals. They work on coasts and in deep seas. They can be found at the water's surface and on the ocean's floor.

Oceans and seas cover 70 percent of Earth's surface. They contain 97 percent of Earth's water and huge numbers of living things. Marine biologists study these plants and animals. They teach, do research, and give speeches. They also write articles for magazines and journals. A lot of research work is done in laboratories. But biologists must also do fieldwork and collect samples. Fieldwork involves traveling. Do you love the sea and enjoy traveling? Marine biology may be a good career choice for you.

Marine science is taught in some high schools and many colleges. College professors usually teach in the fall and spring. They may teach large, general classes on marine biology. They might also teach smaller classes on their special interests. In the summer, professors do research. They apply for grant money from governments or other groups to pay for this research work.

Marine biologists who do not work for colleges find jobs with governments or private companies. They could also work with organizations such as the Ocean Conservancy or Woods Hole Oceanographic Institution. Governments hire marine biologists to study **pollution**, **endangered** species, and the movement and survival of fish. Private companies such as fisheries or tourist attractions also hire marine biologists.

Marine protected areas (MPAs) can also provide jobs for marine biologists. MPAs are regions that receive special protection so that sea life can live there undisturbed by humans. An MPA might be a coastal area, part of an ocean, or another marine location. Marine biologists may be called upon to examine an area chosen to become an MPA. They determine if its size, shape, and location will work for what is needed.

A marine biologist speaks to a group of tourists on a whale-watching trip.

LIFE & CAREER SKILLS

Marine research requires careful planning. Marine biologists need to determine how long it will take to do their projects. They must figure out how much it will cost. They have to decide which tools they need to do the research.

Research is expensive. Applying for grants to cover the cost of research is part of the planning process. Marine biologists need laboratories and office space. They may need to rent ships and hire crews. Project workers are usually paid. Even if students work for free, their employers must pay for travel, shelter, and food expenses.

How do marine biologists handle all of this planning? Being organized and managing time carefully are key to helping research go smoothly. Can you think of ways to become more organized and make the most of your time?

Marine biology jobs require planning skills and lab skills. They also require being able to work within a budget. Communication skills are important, too. Why? Marine biologists use writing skills to apply for grants and to report their findings. They need good public speaking skills to teach classes and to give speeches. Some expert marine biologists even appear on news shows or in documentary films.

Most marine biologists work in groups. They must be able to work well with others—especially when they are working on a ship, where space is limited. When doing fieldwork, marine biologists take on many roles. They become teachers, coaches, teammates, and friends, all at the same time.

21ST CENTURY CONTENT

In 2009, President Barack Obama chose marine biologist Dr. Jane Lubchenco to be the new head of the National Oceanic and Atmospheric Administration. This government agency keeps watch over the world's oceans and atmosphere. Dr. Lubchenco is also a professor at Oregon State University and an award-winning scientist.

In her new position, Dr. Lubchenco will be working to develop ways to stop global climate changes. This is an important issue for the scientific community and all citizens. Marine biologists are among the many scientists working to help solve this global problem.

Two marine biologists discuss an elephant seal with a park ranger in California.

CHAPTER THREE
IT'S NOT ALL DOLPHINS AND WHALES

N early everyone has seen television shows or movies that deal with marine science. Many people also visit aquariums or zoos. TV shows and aquarium visits can

Chemistry classes provide important knowledge for future marine biologists.

lead people to think, "Gee, I'd love to work with dolphins and whales."

But marine biology isn't all about dolphins and whales. TV shows and trips to the aquarium may get you excited about marine biology. But they won't turn you into a marine biologist. Only hard work and years of study can do that.

Study science in high school and college. Chemistry, earth science, and physics provide strong foundations for a marine biologist's education. Why do you need other sciences, such as chemistry, if you want to study clams? You may not be able to determine why a clam population is shrinking without studying the chemical makeup of clamshells. You will also need advanced math and computer skills. Strong writing skills will help you clearly describe your findings.

You will need to learn other skills outside of school. A career in marine biology will lead you to water. Marine biologists often learn how to scuba dive. This helps them reach underwater study sites. Being able to use camera equipment to photograph marine life is another useful skill.

Excited about a career as a marine biologist? Think about attending a camp. Marine science camps give students hands-on experience. Each camp has its own specialty, such as studying whales or diving near coral reefs. Most camps accept young people ages 10 to 18. Camps may help you decide if a career in marine science is for you.

In college you may have the opportunity to help a marine biologist do research. Research is an important part of the education of future marine biologists. Few colleges offer major courses of study in marine biology. Schools that specialize in marine sciences are usually found on the coasts. Marine biologists do not need college degrees specifically in marine biology to work in the field. Many marine biologists have degrees in chemistry, **zoology**, or other subjects.

LIFE & CAREER SKILLS

Students who are interested in a career in marine biology should consider completing an internship. An internship is a chance to work with an expert in your field of interest. Internships give students real-world job experience and help them focus on career paths. They also provide contacts with people working in the students' field of study. Internships show future employers that you took the extra time and effort to learn and improve your skills in your field of study.

Helping professors with their research is a great way to begin a career as a marine biologist.

When looking for a school, begin by investigating the professors and their fields of study. Are you interested in studying elephant seals? Look for schools with professors who are elephant seal experts.

21ST CENTURY CONTENT

Scuba diving might look easy, but there is a lot more to it than just strapping on a mask and jumping into the water. Scuba diving can be very dangerous if you do not take the time to learn how to do it properly. Without the right knowledge, you could end up drowning.

Fortunately, there are many organizations that specialize in teaching people how to scuba dive. The National Association of Underwater Instructors (NAUI), one of the biggest diving organizations in the country, has been teaching people to dive since 1959. You can take classes offered by the NAUI and other organizations in order to receive scuba certification. Then you can dive all you want.

Marine biologists must learn how to use scientific instruments and equipment. They may need to use nets to collect

samples of fish and plankton. They may use devices called salinometers to measure salt levels. Most of the equipment used for sampling and testing can be found in labs. More advanced marine biologists also learn to use underwater submersibles and high-tech underwater video systems.

Finally, most marine work is done from boats. Experience handling a boat will definitely come in handy.

There is a lot to learn if you are going to be a marine biologist. Begin building up the basic skills you will need now. Learn or improve swimming, scuba, and water safety skills. Take every opportunity to learn more about science.

CHAPTER FOUR
A FUTURE IN MARINE BIOLOGY

Some marine biologists do work in zoos and aquariums. But jobs working with seals, sea lions, dolphins, and orcas are rare. The competition for these jobs is high.

Marine biologists collect samples at a fishery to gather information about the animals living there.

Very few jobs in zoos or aquariums involve hands-on contact with marine mammals. The people who train animals for shows are usually not marine biologists.

There are, however, some areas with growing needs for marine biologists. Three growing areas are fishery management, conservation, and **biotechnology**.

Fishery managers work for the government, fishery associations, or fishing companies. They track the numbers of fish, shellfish, and plants in an area. Fishery managers may identify invasive species. Invasive species, such as zebra mussels, destroy the balance of nature in a body of water. Fishery managers use the information they collect to plan which types of fish and shellfish, and how many, can be caught. They help develop plans to control the spread of invasive species.

One good job opportunity for marine biologists is working to build sustainable fisheries. A sustainable fishery is a region where more fish live than are being caught. Fish are an important food source for people all over the world. Most of the world's fisheries suffer from overfishing. Too many fish are being taken. Marine biologists help to manage bodies of water carefully. They help make sure there will be enough food to feed Earth's growing human population.

One good example of fishery management involves the Atlantic cod. By the early 1990s, cod had been fished so heavily that there were almost none left. Countries that fished the North Atlantic agreed not to catch cod anymore. More than a dozen years later, cod populations are still not back to their original numbers. But populations are growing. Current fishery management involves taking cod samples and investigating the growth of the cod population.

Marine biologists do their best to help save endangered species such as the hawksbill sea turtle.

21ST CENTURY CONTENT

Coral reefs are one of the most beautiful features of the world's oceans. But experts are concerned. Increases in water temperatures have caused coral reefs to lose their algae and turn white. This is known as coral bleaching. Coral bleaching can lead to the death of large coral reefs. When the reefs die, many species of fish that depend on the reefs for shelter and food become threatened, too.

Many experts believe global warming is a factor in reef damage. Climate change is a serious global issue in the 21st century. It will remain an issue for years to come. Some marine biologists study the effects of climate change on the world's oceans. What do you think further research on ocean warming will reveal in the future?

Marine conservation biology is another growing field. Many animal and plant species in the oceans are struggling. A marine conservation biologist identifies threatened and endangered species. He or she also develops plans to help the species survive. Some experts study areas called dead zones that are found in some bodies of water. In dead zone waters, there is very little dissolved oxygen. It is very hard for anything to survive in these conditions.

A good example of marine conservation biology is the work being done to preserve coral reefs. One of the joys of being a marine biologist is making new discoveries. In 2006, researchers discovered reefs off the coast of Papua, New Guinea. They have counted 1,200 species of fish there. They have also identified 600 species of reef-building coral. But the discovery was just the beginning of their work. Marine biologists must take samples of each species. They look at the coloring, body structure, and other features of each new species. They must also figure out how to preserve this newly discovered ecosystem.

Another newer, growing specialty for marine biologists is biotechnology. Some people in this field do research on marine organisms to develop and test drugs. Others have invented special coatings to be used on ships and underwater pipes. The coatings can help keep away species such as zebra mussels and barnacles. These species can damage structures or ecosystems.

Fishery management, marine conservation biology, and biotechnology offer jobs that require different levels of schooling. Technicians with bachelor's degrees gather samples and work in laboratories. Marine biologists with doctorates oversee and plan research programs.

The coral reefs of Papua, New Guinea, are filled with a wide variety of marine life.

Jobs in marine biology are changing to meet the needs of a growing human population. The future of marine biology promises to be an exciting one.

If you love science and oceans, then marine biology could be the career for you.

SOME FAMOUS MARINE BIOLOGISTS

Rachel Carson (1907–1964) studied marine biology and earned her master's degree from Johns Hopkins University. Carson is best known for her book *Silent Spring*. An earlier work, *The Sea Around Us,* is still one of the most successful books ever written about the ocean.

Jacques-Yves Cousteau (1910–1997) was a French marine biologist and explorer. Cousteau created more than 120 television documentaries and 50 books about his adventures aboard his research ship, *Calypso*. He worked with engineer Émile Gagnan to invent the self-contained underwater breathing apparatus (better known as scuba). Cousteau was a strong supporter of the environmental movement.

Paul K. Dayton (1941–) is an expert on coastal biology and kelp forests at Scripps Institution of Oceanography in California. He is an active member of the Ocean Conservancy. This environmental group is dedicated to preserving marine life, endangered marine species, and coral reefs.

Michael Moore (1956–) is a Senior Research Specialist at Woods Hole Oceanographic Institution. He specializes in baleen whales. He has devoted himself to ensuring the survival of right whales in the Atlantic Ocean.

Ruth Turner (1914–2000) taught her students that they should "do what sets you on fire." She was a world-renowned marine biologist and Harvard professor. She became the first woman to dive in the *Alvin*, a deep-sea submersible vehicle. Turner was honored as a Woman Pioneer in Oceanography by the Woods Hole Oceanographic Institution.

GLOSSARY

biology (bye-OL-uh-jee) the scientific study of living things

biotechnology (bye-oh-tek-NOL-uh-jee) the use of living things or biological processes to make products

botany (BOT-uh-nee) the study of plants

conservation (kon-sur-VAY-shuhn) the protection and preservation of natural resources and wildlife

coral reefs (KOR-uhl REEFS) rocky structures near the surface of the ocean made up of coral and other material that has solidified

crustaceans (kruhss-TAY-shuhnz) sea creatures with outer skeletons, such as lobsters or shrimp

ecosystem (EE-koh-siss-tuhm) all organisms and the environment in which they live

endangered (en-DAYN-jurd) at risk of becoming extinct

fishery (FISH-ur-ee) a region of water in which fish or seafood is caught

habitats (HAB-uh-tats) places in which animals and plants live

pollution (puh-LOO-shuhn) the presence in air, water, or soil of substances that are harmful or poisonous

rebreathers (ree-BREE-thurz) equipment used in underwater diving

submersible (suhb-MUR-suh-buhl) a vehicle designed for diving or operation underwater

zoology (zoh-OL-uh-jee) the study of animal life

FOR MORE INFORMATION

BOOKS

Baker, Beth. *Sylvia Earle: Guardian of the Sea*. Minneapolis: Lerner Publications Company, 2006.

Thompson, Lisa. *Sea Life Scientist: Have You Got What It Takes to Be a Marine Biologist?* Minneapolis: Compass Point Books, 2008.

Unwin, Mike. *Secrets of the Deep: Marine Biologists*. Chicago: Heinemann Library, 2008.

WEB SITES

Monterey Bay Aquarium: Diving Gear
www.montereybayaquarium.org/lc/activities/diving_gear.asp
Check out the equipment that a marine biologist might use during a diving adventure

Ocean Conservancy
www.oceanconservancy.org/site/PageServer?pagename=home
Discover ways you can be part of the effort to preserve our oceans and the species that live there

Oceanographer/Marine Biologist
kids.earth.nasa.gov/archive/career/oceanographer.html
Learn more about a career as an oceanographer or marine biologist

INDEX

ABOUT THE AUTHOR

Barbara Somervill has written many books about oceans, seas, and the creatures that live in those habitats. Ocean conservation is one of her main interests and she wishes she had studied marine biology as a student.